?WHAT IF...

GIRAFFES

Steve Parker

Copper Beech Books
Brookfield, Connecticut

CONTENTS

© Aladdin Books Ltd 1996
Designed and produced by
Aladdin Books Ltd
28 Percy Street
London W1P 0LD

First published in the United States
in 1996 by Copper Beech Books, an
imprint of The Millbrook Press
2 Old New Milford Road
Brookfield, Connecticut

Editor
Jon Richards

Designed by
David West Children's Books

Designers
Rob Shone and Flick Killerby

Illustrator
John Lobban – B. L. Kearley Ltd

Printed in Belgium

Library of Congress
Cataloging-in-Publication
Data

Parker, Steve.
Giraffes/ by Steve Parker:
illustrated by John Lobban.
p. cm. -- (What if--)
Includes index.
Summary: Explores the world of mammals
by answering such questions as "What if
giraffes had short necks?" "What if a bat
couldn't hear?" and "What if whales could
breathe underwater?"
ISBN 0-7613-0457-6 (lib. bdg.). --
ISBN 0-7613-0472-X (pbk.)
1. Mammals--Miscellanea--Juvenile
literature. [1. Mammals--Miscellanea. 2.
Questions and answers.] I. Lobban, John.
ill. II. Title. III. Series: Parker, Steve. What
if--
QL706.2.P364   1996
599.73'57--dc20   95-50313
CIP
AC

WHAT IF THERE WERE NO INTRODUCTION?

Well you wouldn't be reading this! The *What if...?* books take a look at the world around us from a very unusual angle. Instead of merely explaining what we see from day to day, the books make it a little bit more exciting by asking *What if...* things were very different?

Mammals live in every part of the world. They have been able to adapt to all climates, from polar bears in the frozen lands of the Arctic, to the sperm whales that hunt in the depths of the oceans, and camels that can withstand the searing heat of the desert. They range in size from the smallest mouse to the massive blue whale, and live together in enormous herds or hunt alone. Today over 4,000 species of mammal live with each other and even feed on each other. The state of this planet has been shaped by mammals more than any other group of animal, and by one mammal species in particular – humans.

What if Giraffes...? describes the world of mammals. It explains how they breathe, grow, and feed on each other. It does all this in a way that's easy to remember, by asking what might happen if... things were different!

WHAT IF GIRAFFES HAD SHORT NECKS?

Some do! The okapi is a type of giraffe found in the tropical rain forests of central Africa. Unlike its taller relative, the giraffe of the African plains, all of its food is within easy reach among the lush jungle vegetation. As a result, it does not need the long neck of the plains giraffe. The tree branches of the African plains are found well above the ground, so the giraffe needs a long neck to stretch up and eat the leaves that can be over 19 ft (6 m) high. The giraffe's unique feature has evolved over years of evolution, so that it is now perfectly suited to its way of life.

Designed by committee

The odd shape of the giraffe, with its big head, long neck, long front legs, and short back legs, has often been described as an animal put together by a committee. However, the peculiar body has evolved naturally over time. The result may look odd, but it works.

Lookout post

Not only does the giraffe's tall neck allow it to reach the highest branches, it lets it see over long distances. High above the grassy plains, the giraffe can spot danger, such as a bush fire or a prowling hunter, or even new trees to eat, from several miles away.

Okapi

All creatures great and small

Just as the neck of the giraffe has developed over millions of years, so nature has created a whole host of different mammals. There are currently over 4,000 species of mammal, ranging from enormous whales to tiny mice, and from peaceful cows to aggressive tigers. Each of these has developed its own method of survival, involving a bizarre array of physical features. These include the hump of a camel, the stripes of a zebra, or the trunk of an elephant. All of these strange-looking features have evolved to help the animal survive in its environment.

The long and short of it

A giraffe, like all other mammals, including the okapi, has only seven vertebrae in its neck. However, these neck bones are greatly elongated (stretched), allowing the giraffe's head to stand way above the ground.

Giraffe

What if dinosaurs were still alive?

Then we would not be here! Mammals and dinosaurs first appeared at the same time, about 200 million years ago. However, it was the dinosaurs who were first to develop and rule the Earth. Mammals could not compete, and they had to be very small to survive. Then, mysteriously, the dinosaurs died out about 65 million years ago, and mammals were able to develop into their many and various forms (see above). If the dinosaurs were still here, then the largest mammal would probably be about the size of a cat.

WHAT IF A LEOPARD COULD CHANGE ITS SPOTS?

A leopard's spots are designed to break up its outline and keep it hidden, especially when it's crawling through the long grass, or lying on a tree branch. Many mammals have this type of camouflage – both the hunted and the hunters, including tigers. If these animals were brightly colored, or if they had strange patterns on their fur, they would stand out, and enemies could spot them at once!

Dappled deer

Adult red deer tend to graze in open areas. But baby red deer, called fawns, hide by lying still among ferns or heather, under a bush, or in a thicket. The sunlight shining through the leaves creates light and shadow below. So the fawn's coat has similar light and dark patches to conceal it in the dappled sunlight.

What if a polar bear had no fur coat?

Its naked, pinkish body would show up clearly against the white background of snow and ice. So the polar bear would have trouble trying to sneak up on seals to eat, and it would get very hungry. It would also be extremely cold. This is another job of a mammal's hairy coat – to protect against the cold (or heat, as in the case of a camel). The polar bear's fur coat is extremely thick and warm, as well as extra white. Without it, the bear would quickly freeze to death.

Stop blubbering!

All mammals have a layer of a soft, fatty substance just under the skin, covering the muscles and other inner parts. When this is very thick, it's called *blubber*. It makes the seal's body smooth and sleek, and acts as a store of energy should food ever get scarce.

However, its major role is as a wraparound blanket of fat to help the fur keep out the cold, especially when the animal is swimming in the icy seawater. Some seals can have a layer blubber that is more than 4 in (10 cm) thick.

Fur
Skin
Blubber
Muscle

Skinny seal
A blubberless seal would not only look very thin, it would very quickly freeze to death in the cold seas that it swims through.

What if mammals had spears and armor?

Some do – the porcupine has spines and the armadillo has armor-plating. The porcupine has normal mammal fur and also very thick, sharp-tipped, spearlike hairs growing from the skin. These are quills which are only attached loosely to the skin. The porcupine can flick its tail and throw off the quills into an unwary attacker's face.

The armadillo has a covering of small bone plates embedded in horny skin, with patches of tough skin and hairs between them. The plates hang down over the creature's head, sides, legs, and tail. When threatened, the armadillo can roll up into an armor-plated ball.

WHAT IF A BAT COULDN'T HEAR?

Clicks

Echoes

Bat sonar

The bat's sound pulses are so high-pitched that you or I couldn't hear them. However, a bat's hearing is so sensitive, it can hear these clicks and their echoes. The bat can find its way and catch its flying food even in complete darkness. The system is like radar, but with sound waves instead of radio waves. It's known as sonar or echolocation.

It would fly through the dark night – and crash into things! Mammals possess an amazing array of senses to detect the outside world. Hearing is only one of these. They are able to see in very poor light, smell the very faintest odors, taste an enormous variety of different foods, and detect touches and vibrations that are as light as a feather.

Dolphin sonar

Predatory members of the whale group, such as dolphins and killer whales, have a sonar system like the bat's (above). The sound pulses are concentrated, or focused, into a beam by a large lump in the forehead, the melon.

melon

What if whales could sing?

All whales make underwater sounds, varying from shrill clicks and squeaks and squawks, to haunting low moans and groans. Beluga and humpback whales are so noisy that their calls can be heard underwater more than 125 miles (200 km) away. The "songs" of a whale can last between 6 and 35 minutes, and are used by the whales to communicate with each other.

Nighttime eye-shine

If you've ever shone a flashlight into a cat's eyes, you will have seen that they appeared to glow in the dark. A cat's eye has a mirrorlike layer inside, the tapetum. Light rays come into the eye and some are detected by the light-sensitive layer, the retina. Others pass through the retina, bounce off the tapetum, and get sensed by the retina on the way out. This gives the eye two chances to detect light rays. Other nocturnal (nighttime) animals, such as opossums, have this too.

The pupil opens wider in dark conditions, to let in more light.

The retina detects light and turns it into nerve signals, which go to the brain.

The tapetum is a layer behind the retina. It reflects the light back onto the retina.

What if a lion had eyes on the side of its head?

It would leap at its prey, and probably miss! Most hunters, such as seals, cats, and foxes, have two forward-facing eyes at the front of the head. This gives them overlapping fields of vision (right), and allows them to judge distances well, for pursuit and pounce. Most hunted mammals, such as deer, zebras, and rabbits, have eyes on the sides of their head. Although this means that they can't judge distances well, it does give them a good overall view for spotting any predators that may be creeping up on them (right).

Something in the air

Dogs sniff everything, from the food they eat, to other dogs, especially when it is time to mate. The scent in the air enters the nose and attaches to an organ called the *olfactory bulb*. This is very large and very sensitive in a dog's nose. It then sends signals to the brain.

Olfactory bulb

WHAT IF MAMMALS LAID EGGS?

You would need very strong eggshells! Fortunately, very few mammals actually lay eggs in the same way as birds and reptiles. Those that do, such as the bizarre-looking duck-billed platypus, are called *monotremes*. Other mammals give birth to live young. Some, called *marsupials*, carry the young in a pouch, while the rest keep the immature baby within a part of their body called the *womb*. Here it can grow and develop.

This period of time when the baby mammal is inside the mother is called the *gestation period*. Its length varies greatly, depending on the size of the animal. The human gestation period is about 270 days. The Asiatic elephant can carry its young for an astonishing 760 days. However, the Virginian opossum is pregnant for as little as eight days!

Egg-cellent parents!

There are only three species of mammal that actually lay eggs. These are the duck-billed platypus (above), the long-beaked echidna (right), and the short-beaked echidna, which all live in Australasia. The duck-billed platypus usually lays two eggs in an underground den. These eggs are covered in a tough leathery shell to protect them.

After about ten to twelve days in the den, the babies hatch from their eggs and feed on milk. This is produced by special glands on the mother (see page 12).

Womb   Ovaries

Eggs without shells

Although most mammals don't lay eggs like
birds or reptiles, they all (including humans)
produce tiny, microscopic eggs from
organs inside the female, called *ovaries*.
After mating, these eggs may be
fertilized with sperm from the male,
they embed themselves into an area
of the mother's womb. The baby
grows here, protected from the
outside world and fed by
nutrients that pass from the
mother's blood. These nutrients
are passed from the mother to
the baby through an organ
called the *placenta*, and along
the umbilical cord. Once the
baby has developed enough, it
is born. It passes from the
womb, through the birth canal,
and out into the world.

Baby elephant

Birth canal

What if a kangaroo didn't have a pouch on its belly?

It would have to find some other way of carrying
around its young. Kangaroos give birth to very
immature, furless babies. The tiny creature has to
crawl through its mother's fur, into the pouch,
where it attaches itself to one of four milk teats.

The pouch is called a *marsupium*, and
mammals that have this are referred to as
marsupials. These include possums, opossums,
koalas, and wombats.

WHAT IF COWS HAD NO UDDERS?

The udders of a cow hold the milk-producing glands, known as *mammary glands*. Mammals are the only animals to have these milk-producing organs to feed their young. The young cow merely has to suck on its mother's teats to be fed with a rich supply of nutrients. These are essential for the calf during the first months of its life. Without udders and teats, the young calves would starve, and we would be without milk to pour over our cereal in the morning!

Milk glands

Udders

What if we drank seal's milk?

We would get very fat indeed! The milk that different mammals produce varies greatly, depending on the needs of the young animal. Seals need to put on a thick layer of fat, called *blubber*, to keep them warm in the cold sea (see page 7). Because of this, the milk that seal mothers produce is very high in fat. Cow's and human's has only 4.5%, while seal's milk contains 53.2% fat – not very good if you're on a diet!

Bouncing delivery

When an infant kangaroo (joey) first reaches its mother's pouch after birth, it attaches itself to one of four teats (see page 11). The teat then swells and fixes the joey firmly within the pouch. It remains clamped to the teat for about two months, by which time the mouth has grown enough to release the joey. After another four months, the joey is old enough to leave the pouch, but it still continues to feed on its original teat, even climbing into the pouch when it needs a rest.

Meanwhile, another baby kangaroo may have been born. This, too, will have crawled into its mother's pouch and will be suckling on a different teat. Kangaroos can therefore carry two joeys in their pouch at the same time.

Feeding time
As the joey grows, the milk it drinks from the teat changes. At birth, the milk is very rich in nutrients, which decline as it gets older. With two babies feeding in the pouch, the mother will be producing two different types of milk!

What if baby mammals were left to fend for themselves?

They would become easy food for predators such as wolves, lions, and eagles!

Without any parents to take care of them, baby mammals would have to learn to hunt, hide, and forage in order to reach adulthood. Fortunately, mammal parents take more care of their young than any other animals, ensuring that plenty of them get to old age. The parents' first concern is to feed their young. This is done by supplying milk from the mother. They must also teach their babies how to find food, either by hunting or grazing.

As the young grow, the parents must also protect them from any predators that are after an easy snack. This doesn't mean that baby mammals are completely helpless. Some, like antelope, are able to run almost as soon as they are born.

WHAT IF A LION HAD NO PRIDE?

Solitary cats

Apart from the lion, all 34 other kinds of cats – from tigers to wildcats – are mainly solitary. They live and hunt alone. Only during the breeding season when a male and a female are together, and when a mother is with her cubs, do these cats have any company.

It would be very lonely. Lions are the only cats that live in groups, or prides. As with any group of animals, each of the lions has a different role. The females hunt for food and bring up the babies, or cubs. The males defend the females of the pride and the area of land where they live, called the *territory*, from rival males and other prides of lions.

Elephants on parade

When moving from place to place, elephants may walk in a long line, like soldiers on parade. The herd is led by the oldest female, or cow, the matriarch. The rest of the herd, including her sisters, daughters, and their babies, rely on her to find food and water.

Rival male

A fully grown male will leave his original pride. He will then wander alone for a while, then try to join another pride, so that he can mate with the females, and father offspring. But first he must challenge the pride's leader.

Leader of the pride

The chief male of the pride defends his females and territory fiercely. He fluffs up his mane to look large and strong, and growls loud and long. He tries to repel the rival by fright first. If this doesn't work, it may come to a real fight!

Female hunters

The older, experienced females are the pride's main hunters. They work together to chase and separate a herd of zebra and wildebeest, then they run down a young, old, or sick member. However, they will let the pride-leading male eat first.

Safety in numbers

Many large plant-eating mammals form herds with others of their kind. Sometimes they form mixed herds too, like zebra with wildebeest and gazelles. These herds can number from a handful to many thousands of animals.

There are many noses and pairs of eyes and ears that can detect any approaching danger. If one herd member spots trouble, it can warn the others. Should a predator approach too closely, the herd panics and runs. The hunter then finds it hard to single out one victim from the blur of bodies, heads, legs, and stripes that flash past very quickly.

Trooping baboons

The baboon is a type of monkey that spends much of its time on the ground. Baboons dwell in groups called *troops*, which can be subdivided into bands, clans, and family groups. The troops can number up to 250 baboons. These are based around the mothers and their children. There are a few males, and the biggest, most senior of these lead the troop from danger or defend it against predators, such as the leopard.

Lion cubs
Females with young cubs guard their offspring and feed them on mother's milk. However, danger may come with a rival male, which will kill any existing cubs if it takes over the pride so that its own can be reared.

Young males
The growing males stay with the pride, as long as they do not threaten the leading male. When they want to have any cubs of their own, then they must either challenge the leading male, or leave and take over another pride.

Summer

Fall   Spring

Winter

WHAT IF A SQUIRREL DIDN'T STORE ITS NUTS?

It might starve during the long winter months, when food is hard to find. Many mammals gather food during times of plenty, to hide away and keep, and eat when food is scarce. Squirrels collect fall nuts, such as oak acorns and hazel cobs, and bury them in the ground. Later, the squirrel is only able to find about one-quarter of the nuts it stored, but that's enough to see it through the winter months.

The big sleep

Squirrels and many other small mammals sleep for long periods in winter, when the weather is cold and food is scarce. By going to sleep, they are able to slow down the speed at which their body works (see below) and so save energy. To prepare for winter, the mammal has to fatten itself up during fall, before it goes to sleep.

Life in the fast lane

Different mammals live to different ages. In general, bigger mammals live longer. They need the time to grow from a baby to full size. Small mammals, however, live their life faster. Their body processes, such as heartbeat and breathing, are quicker. A shrew's heart beats 800 times a minute, even when it is resting. An elephant's beats a mere 25 times a minute. All this activity and action mean smaller animals "wear out" and die sooner. A shrew aged six months is very old, whereas elephants may live to more than 70 years.

Gliding and Flying

A few small mammals are capable of gliding and even flying. Flying squirrels and gliding possums can swoop, using a flap of skin between their legs, like the wings of a glider.

However, bats are the only mammals that can truly fly. During millions of years of evolution, the bat's arms have developed into wings. The long finger bones hold open a very thin, leathery wing membrane, which the bat flaps to stay in the air.

Membrane

Finger

Going underground

While some small mammals live in the trees, or swoop and soar through the sky, others have chosen to spend their lives underground. A mole tunnels by scraping and pushing aside the soil with its large, powerful, spade-shaped front paws. These have very big, strong claws, like the spikes of a pickax. The mole pushes up extra soil here and there, forming molehills. Tunnels radiate from a central nest, called the *fortress*.

This mammal spends most of its life underground, roaming its existing tunnels and digging new ones, to find food such as earthworms and soil grubs.

Working on the nightshift

Many small mammals, such as bats and rats, are active mainly when it is dark. These nighttime animals are called *nocturnal*. Other mammals, such as monkeys and squirrels are active mostly by day. They are *diurnal*.

Night mammals usually have large eyes to see in the dark, keen noses to smell, extremely sensitive hearing to sense the slightest sound and large whiskers to feel their way. Day mammals, like the bear, only need small eyes to see in the bright sunlight. If these daytime mammals went out in the dark, they would never be able to find their way.

WHAT IF AN ELEPHANT HAD NO TRUNK?

The long trunk is one of the main features of the animal, and it couldn't survive without it. The trunk is the nose and upper lip, that have joined together and grown very long. The elephant uses its trunk for many vital actions, especially eating and drinking. Without a trunk, this plant-eater would not be able to pick up grass and leaves to eat. It also uses the trunk to smell, breathe, feel, and to suck up water. If the elephant crosses a deep river, it can even use its trunk as a snorkel!

Trunk call

The hairy tip of the trunk is very sensitive to touch. The two holes are nostrils that lead to the long nose tube. Through this the elephant breathes and trumpets its calls. Muscles bend the trunk in any direction.

Sniffing and smelling

Elephants lift their trunks high to sniff the air for predators, fire, and other dangers, and to catch the scent of their herd and other creatures. They also smell food before eating it.

The daily grind

Long, thin, sharp, fang-shaped teeth are good for catching, killing, and ripping up meaty prey – but they are no good for chewing or grinding up leaves, grass, fruits, and other plant parts. Herbivores (plant-eaters) need wide, broad, fairly flat teeth to mash and pulp their food thoroughly. This is because plants are made from tough fibers that need to be broken down, so that a herbivore's intestines can extract the nutrients.

Feeding

The elephant has a short neck, so its head cannot reach down to the ground or up to the trees. But the trunk can. It curls around juicy grasses and leaves, rips them off, and stuffs them into its mouth.

Communicating

Elephants touch and stroke their fellow herd members, to greet them and keep up their friendships. They also trumpet and make noises with the help of their trunk. These forms of communication are very important to the herd.

Chewing the cud

Some mammals are able to swallow their food quickly, and then bring it up again to chew over slowly. They are called *ruminants*. They include cows, antelope, and llamas.

When the food is first swallowed it goes into the rumen, the first part of the four-chambered stomach (below). The animal can then bring up this half-digested food, called *cud*, to chew over more leisurely. The cud is then swallowed into the reticulum, and then into the intestines.

Drinking and bathing

The trunk's long nasal tubes allow the elephant to suck up enormous amounts of water. This can then be flung over its back when it wishes to cool off at a watering hole. Alternatively, the elephant may be thirsty, and then it will empty its trunk into its mouth to take a drink.

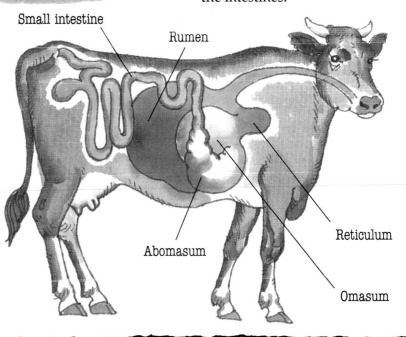

Small intestine

Rumen

Abomasum

Reticulum

Omasum

WHAT IF A TIGER HAD NO TEETH?

It would soon go hungry and starve. The tiger uses its claws to catch and scratch prey. But it needs its teeth to deliver the deadly bites, and to slice the meat off the bones for eating. The tiger has two main kinds of teeth for these jobs. The long, sharp canines or "fangs" are at the front of the mouth. They stab, wound, and skin the victim, making it bleed, suffocate, and die.

The large, ridge-edged carnassial teeth at the back of the mouth come together like the blades of scissors when the tiger closes its jaws. These very strong teeth carve off and slice up the meat, and can even crunch gristle (cartilage) and soft bones.

Carnassial teeth

Canine teeth

Purr-fect claws

A cat's claws are vital for its survival in the wild. With these incredibly sharp weapons, the hunter can slash, stab, and pin prey that will become its food. However, these deadly claws need to be kept razor sharp for the next kill. To ensure this, most cats can withdraw, or retract, their claws into sheaths in the toes.

This allows the cat to run, walk, and jump without scraping its sharp talons along the ground. It keeps them sharp, unbroken, and clean. It keeps them from getting blunt or getting tangled in twigs, grass, bark, and other things. When the cat needs its claws to climb a tree or to slash and pin its prey, it makes them stick out of the toes.

Claws indoors
The cat's claw is equivalent to your fingernail or toenail. But the claw can swing or pivot on its toe bone. A muscle in the lower leg pulls on a long, stringlike tendon that is attached to the bone and claw. This pulls the sharp claw out of its protective sheath.

Bone

Tendon

Claw

Plant-eating carnivore

When the giant panda of China was first discovered, it posed a problem to scientists. It has the sharp, fanglike teeth of a carnivore (meat-eater), and is indeed a close relative of the meat-eating raccoon. However, its diet consists almost solely of bamboo shoots. Even though it can eat meat, the panda chooses the young shoots of this type of grass. Unfortunately, bamboo is very low in nutritional value. As a result, it must spend nearly all of its time sitting around, lazily eating in order to consume enough to survive.

Highly-sprung hunter

The fastest hunter on land owes its speed to its flexible backbone. Without this powerful spring running along its spine, the cheetah would not be able to catch and kill the nimble prey that it hunts, such as gazelle and springbok.

As this big cat sprints, the spine flexes, stretching the body out, and allowing the legs to cover even more distance with each stride. This makes the cheetah the world's fastest runner, at over 60 mph (100 km/h).

As the cheetah's legs come together, the spine bends up in the middle.

As the cheetah extends its legs, the spine flattens and arches backward.

As a result the legs can stretch further apart, letting the cheetah run faster.

WHAT IF WHALES COULD BREATHE UNDERWATER?

"Thar she blows!" – whale hunters used to shout this when they spotted a whale coming to the surface, blowing out a plume of sea spray and air from its lungs. A whale must do this every so often in order to breathe. Whales are like us, with a pair of lungs inside their bodies. This means that they can only breathe in air, and must hold their breath underwater – if they tried to breathe underwater, they would drown!

In order to stay underwater forever they would need gills, like a fish, which can take oxygen from water. Then they would never need to come to the surface for air. But then they wouldn't be mammals at all.

Without the aid of breathing apparatus, humans have only been able to dive down to around 425 feet (130 m).

Lungs

Blowhole

Some whales, such as sperm whales, can stay underwater for up to 2 hours, and can dive down to nearly 9,900 feet (3,000 m) in order to hunt for food.

What if seals had a pair of legs?

They do! But they look very different from ours. Seal's legs have the same bones as other mammals' legs, but they have evolved over millions of years in order to adapt to their underwater lifestyle.

However, not all seal legs are the same. Seals are split into two groups – true seals and eared seals. True seals use their back legs for swimming and can only drag them across the land. Eared seals, on the other hand, do not swim with their hind limbs, but can use them to waddle about on the beach.

Real-life mermaids

When early sailors first spotted the gentle-swimming manatees and dugongs that live in tropical rivers and coastal waters, they thought they had seen mermaids. Instead of being half-human and half-fish, these placid creatures are mammals which graze on the vegetation that grows on river and seabeds, or floats along the water's surface.

Narwhal

Underwater duelist

Like the tusk of an elephant, the "horn" of a male narwhal is made from a tooth that grows in a spiral from the upper-left part of the jaw. These "horns" can grow up to 10 feet (3 m) long. Many uses have been suggested for this strange feature, from icebreaker to food spear.

The most likely explanation is that male narwhals use them to fight each other, sometimes inflicting dangerous injuries.

Dugong

WHAT IF HUMANS COULD GRIP WITH THEIR FEET?

You could hang upside down from a tree, and do all kinds of other exciting activities. But you might not be able to run and jump so easily. Human feet are designed for walking, and human hands for holding. Our monkey and ape cousins spend most of their time in trees, so they don't need to walk. Instead, all their limbs can grip like hands. Some monkeys are even able to grip with their tails!

Orangutan

These great orange apes live in the densest, steamiest rainforests of Southeast Asia. They rarely come to the ground, and they can bend their legs at almost any angle from the body.

What if apes could stand upright?

One close cousin of the great apes spends most of its time upright. That's us! The true great apes, however, are not able to stand for long. The gorilla spends much of the day on the ground. It usually walks on all fours, on its feet and hand-knuckles. Males sometimes stand upright and charge, if they are threatened by an intruder. Chimps and orangutans can walk upright in order to carry things like fruit, sticks, or rocks. But they can only keep this up for short distances.

Gibbon

The gibbons of Southeast Asia are the champion tree-swingers. They hang from branches by their hooklike hands and powerful arms, and move by swinging from tree to tree with astonishing speed. Because of this, their arms are much longer and stronger than their legs.

Potto

This primate from Africa looks like a small bear. It moves very slowly through the trees.

Tarsier

The tarsier's huge eyes show that it comes out mainly at night. It can leap by its back legs to another branch 7 feet (2 m) away! It feeds on small animals and insects.

Flag-waving primate

Lemurs are primates from the large island of Madagascar, off the eastern coast of Africa. They can run across the ground or leap through trees with equal ease. When they aren't leaping about or searching for food, lemurs like to bask in the warm sun.

The ring-tailed lemur (below) signals to its troop by sight and smell. It waves its black-and-white, ring-patterned tail, like a flag. This is covered with a special scent that the lemur produces from glands on its shoulders.

Spider monkey

The spider monkey has a gripping tail, to help it move through the trees. Without it, the monkey might slip and crash to the floor.

What if apes could use tools?

Humans are not the only animals to use tools, many others use them as well. The great apes are tool-users, especially the chimp. It makes a tool by stripping the leaves off a twig, then pokes the twig into a termite mound, to dig out the termites for a snack. Animal tools are natural objects like leaves, stones, and twigs. They haven't figured out how to use any power tools, yet!

WHAT IF SHEEP HAD NO WOOL?

Humans have been using animals, such as sheep, cows, and pigs, for thousands of years. These domesticated mammals have been supplying us with meat, milk, and materials. If sheep didn't have any wool, then not only would they be cold, but we would not be able to use their fleece to make our woolen clothes.

Sheep's wool is sheared, washed, cleaned, and woven into clothes, rugs, and many other woolen products.

Mammal products

Mammals produce a wide range of products that humans use directly or convert into other substances. The milk of mammals such as cows, goats, and camels is made into butter, cheese, and yogurt. We eat the muscles, or red meat. We crush and melt bones and hard pieces into glues and fertilizers. Clothes and textiles are made from the wool (mammal fur) of sheep, goats, vicunas, rabbits, rodents, and many others.

Chamois leather is the skin of the chamois, a type of goat-antelope. It is very soft, flexible, and absorbent.

A-hunting we will go

Although hunting for sport takes place in many places throughout the world, several groups of people rely on hunting mammals to survive. For example, the Inuit (Eskimo) of the far north hunt whales, walruses, and seals for their meat, bones and fur to make food, clothing, and utensils.

Bizarre pets

For as long as people have been using mammals for food, they have also been keeping them as pets. Since this time we have bred many different animals. Some of these were bred for their ability to work, such as sheepdogs, but now they are mainly for company or for show. The result has been some very strange-looking animals, such as the bulldog, whose nose is so short that it can only breathe through its mouth, the hairless sphinx cat, and the shaggy rough-haired guinea pig.

Cows provide most of our ordinary leather. They also give us a lot of meat and make most of the milk that we drink.

Pigs yield many products, from meat to pigskin for shoes. They are used to make drugs and body organs for transplants.

Arks or prisons?

Zoos have become the center of debate between many groups of people. Some people believe that keeping wild animals captive in cages is cruel.

However, zoos can play a positive role in the conservation of many species. Conservationists can breed rare creatures such as the giant panda, golden lion tamarin, and rhinoceros, to release them back into the wild and save them from extinction.

Zoos have not always been successful in saving species. Some animals, such as the quagga from Africa and the thylacine from Australia, have become extinct, despite having some specimens kept in zoos

Rhinoceros

Giant panda

Quagga

Golden lion tamarin

WHAT IF MAMMALS HAD NEVER EXISTED?

Mammals are quite recent arrivals on the world's stage. Although the first appeared 200 million years ago, they did not flourish until fifty million years ago. Since then they have come to dominate the world. If they never been around, things would be very different.

Reptiles

Without mammals to compete with, the reptiles may well have recovered from the extinction of the dinosaurs, to rule the world again!

Arthropods

Spiders and scorpions are some of the oldest animals. Without mammals around to eat them and their food, there might be more arthropods around.

Amphibians

A lot of amphibians are eaten by mammals. Without them around, there would probably be a lot more frogs in the world.

Worms

Some mammals, such as moles and hedgehogs, feed on worms. Without mammals, worms could tunnel through the soil without being eaten.

What if there were no sea mammals?

Mammals are some of the largest creatures swimming throughout the waters of the world. Whales, dolphins, seals, and otters eat a massive amount of fish, krill, and other sea animals. Without mammals, there would certainly be a lot more fish around (especially because humans eat a vast quantity of fish every day!).

Other predators, such as sharks, would need to find alternative sources of food. However, there are plenty of other fish to eat. In fact, mammals only make up a small percentage of sea creatures, so if they had never existed, they wouldn't be missed all that much.

Insects

Some insects, such as mosquitoes, feed on the blood of mammals. Without mammals, they would have to find something else that they could eat.

Birds

Several species have been hunted to extinction by mammals, such as the diatryma and the elephant bird. If mammals had never been around, these birds could still be alive.

Molluscs

These creatures are incredibly successful and numerous in the sea, from sea snails to cuttlefish and squid. They provide food for both whales and dolphins. If they weren't eaten, they would be even more successful.

On top of the world

Without mammals there wouldn't be any humans. Scientists have pondered whether any other group of animal could produce a species as intelligent as ourselves. The favorites to fill the empty space might be the reptiles. They have already dominated the Earth once, during the reign of the dinosaurs. Some believe if they did not die out, then the world could be populated by highly intelligent, bipedal (two legged) lizards.

FACTFILE

The largest mammal, and the largest animal ever, is the blue whale. This can grow 110 feet (30 m) long and weigh an astonishing 190 tons!

The largest mammal on land is the African elephant, which can stand over 13 feet (4 m) high and weigh over 12 tons.

It is claimed that some armadillos, opossums, and sloths spend up to 80% of their time asleep. On the other hand, the Dall's porpoise is said to never sleep at all!

The smallest land mammal is the Etruscan shrew which weighs only 0.05 ounces (1.5 g) and is only 2.2 inches (60 mm) long.

The largest herd of animals on record are those of the springbok. One herd observed took three days to pass one spot!

The tailless tenrec of Madagascar and the Comoro Islands can give birth to over 30 babies in one go.

Kangaroos are able to jump over fences 10 feet (3 m) high, and to long-jump up to 41 feet (12.5 m).

The fastest long-distance runner is the pronghorn antelope of the United States. It can run at 35 mph (56 km/h) for more than 4 miles (6 km).

In contrast, the three-toed sloth of South America can only travel about 6 feet (1.8 m) in an hour, but can, if pushed, reach 15 feet (4.6 m) per minute.

Apart from humans, the mammals to reach the oldest age are Asiatic elephants. One, called Rajah from Sri Lanka, was said to be 81 years old when he died.

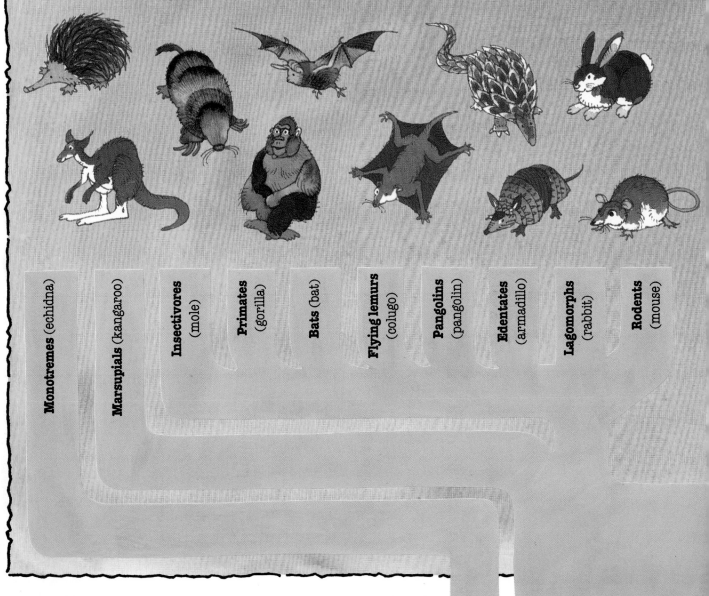

Monotremes (echidna)

Marsupials (kangaroo)

Insectivores (mole)

Primates (gorilla)

Bats (bat)

Flying lemurs (colugo)

Pangolins (pangolin)

Edentates (armadillo)

Lagomorphs (rabbit)

Rodents (mouse)

GLOSSARY

Blubber
A thick layer of fat, just under the skin, found in sea mammals, such as whales and seals. It keeps them warm in the cold sea.

Diurnal
An animal that is awake during the day and sleeps at night, is referred to as a diurnal creature.

Evolution
The changes that all living things have undergone in order to adapt to their environment over time.

Fur
A coat of hair that covers many mammals and keeps them warm (and cool!).

Herd
A group of animals, which can range from a small family group to many millions of different creatures.

Hibernation
The deep "sleep" that some creatures undergo during the cold winter months.

Mammary gland
The milk-producing gland found on all female mammals.

Marsupial
Animals who give birth to very undeveloped young. These young then develop and grow inside the mother's pouch.

Monotreme
An egg-laying mammal.

Nocturnal
A creature that is asleep during the day and awake at night is referred to as nocturnal.

Predator
An animal that actively hunts, kills, and eats other creatures.

Primate
The group of animals including monkeys, apes, and humans.

Ruminant
A plant-eating mammal with a four-chambered stomach, that is capable of regurgitating its food to chew over and so aid digestion.

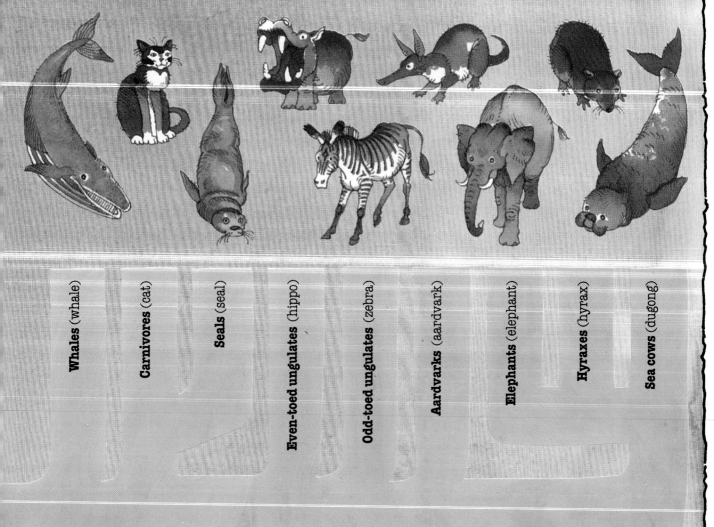

Whales (whale) **Carnivores** (cat) **Seals** (seal) **Even-toed ungulates** (hippo) **Odd-toed ungulates** (zebra) **Aardvarks** (aardvark) **Elephants** (elephant) **Hyraxes** (hyrax) **Sea cows** (dugong)

INDEX

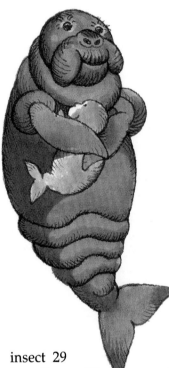